Nita Mehta's New Chinese

Vegetarian

Nita Mehta
B.Sc. (Home Science), M.Sc. (Food and Nutrition), Gold Medalist

Tanya Mehta

SNAB
Publishers Pvt Ltd

Nita Mehta's
New Chinese – Vegetarian

© Copyright 2003-2008 **SNAB** Publishers Pvt Ltd

WORLD RIGHTS RESERVED. The contents—all recipes, photographs and drawings are original and copyrighted. No portion of this book shall be reproduced, stored in a retrieval system or transmitted by any means, electronic, mechanical, photocopying, recording or otherwise, without the written permission of the publishers.

While every precaution is taken in the preparation of this book, the publisher and the author assume no responsibility for errors or omissions. Neither is any liability assumed for damages resulting from the use of information contained herein.

TRADEMARKS ACKNOWLEDGED. Trademarks used, if any, are acknowledged as trademarks of their respective owners. These are used as reference only and no trademark infringement is intended upon. Ajinomoto (monosodium glutamate, MSG) is a trademark of Aji-no-moto company of Japan. Use it sparingly if you must as a flavour enhancer.

4th Print 2008
ISBN 978-81-7869-065-0

Food Styling and Photography: **SNAB**

Layout and laser typesetting:

National Information Technology Academy
3A/3, Asaf Ali Road
New Delhi-110002
☎ 23252948

Published by:

Publishers Pvt. Ltd.
3A/3 Asaf Ali Road,
New Delhi - 110002
Tel: 23252948, 23250091
Telefax: 91-11-23250091

Contributing Writers:
Anurag Mehta
Subhash Mehta

Editorial & Proofreading:
Rakesh
Ramesh

Editorial and Marketing office:
E-159, Greater Kailash-II, N.Delhi-48
Fax: 91-11-29225218, 29229558
Tel: 91-11-29214011, 29218727, 29218574
E-Mail: nitamehta@email.com
nitamehta@nitamehta.com
Website: http://www.nitamehta.com
Website: http://www.snabindia.com

Distributed by:
THE VARIETY BOOK DEPOT
A.V.G. Bhavan, M 3 Con Circus,
New Delhi - 110 001
Tel: 23417175, 23412567; Fax: 23415335
Email: varietybookdepot@rediffmail.com

Printed by:
BRIJBASI ART PRESS LTD.

Rs. 89/-

Picture on cover:	*Half Balls and Veggies in Sauce 70*
Picture on page 1:	*Mongolian Lotus Stem 52*
	Glass Noodles with Sesame Paste 94
	Corn Wheels 24
Picture on page 2:	*Broccoli in Garlic Butter Sauce 56*
Picture on backcover:	*Cauliflower in Pepper Sauce 50*

Introduction

"New Chinese" offers the latest Chinese dishes now available at good Chinese restaurants. Chinese food is full of flavour and the texture of vegetables in every dish is crisp. Keeping this in mind, the recipes have been put down in a very orderly manner, so as to retain the colour and crispiness of vegetables.

The specialty starter "Dim Sums" with a special dipping sauce will set the mood rolling for the party. The main course has lots to offer. Our favourite Paneer or Tofu in a special Fennel flavoured Sauce and the Stir Fried Okra in Hoisin Sauce will make a perfect meal with Pepper Fried Rice and Pea Cinnamon Noodles. Honey Crispies served with ice cream at the end of the meal will leave your guests in awe of you and waiting for the next invitation.

Enjoy the taste of China, all cooked in a simple delicious manner.

Nita Mehta

About The Recipes
What's In A Cup?
INDIAN CUP
1 teacup = 200 ml liquid
AMERICAN CUP
1 cup = 240 ml liquid (8 oz.)
The recipes in this book were tested with the Indian teacup which holds 200 ml liquid.

Contents

Ingredients used for Chinese Dishes 10

Starters & Dips 13

Kimchi Salad 13
Crispy Cinnamon Cauliflower 14
Red Sesame Dip 17
Momos 18
Honey Rice Balls 22
Corn Rolls 24
Crunchy Bread Balls 26
Fried Rice Triangles 28
Sweet Chilli Dip 31

Soups 32

Fresh Vegetable Stock 32
Quick Vegetable Stock 33
Lemon Coriander Soup 34
Manchow Soup 36
Mushroom Ginger Crispy Rice Soup 40
Stir fried Vegetable Soup 42

Main Dishes 43

Potato Strings in Ginger Sauce 43
Babycorn Aniseed 45
Cauliflower in Pepper Sauce 50
Mongolian Lotus Stem 52
Stir fried Snow Peas/Beans 54
Broccoli in Garlic Butter Sauce 56
Steak & Mung Beans 58
Paneer in 5 Spice Powder 61
Kung Pao Corn 64
Hoisin Stir Fry Okra 68
Half Balls & Veggies in Sauce 70
Billy Kee Mushroom in Sauce 72
Moons in Almond Sauce 74

New Chinese

Shredded Aubergine in Sweet & Sour Sauce 78
Veggies in Caramelized Sauce 80
Garlic Honey Cottage Cheese 82
Schzewan Vegetables 84

Rice & Noodles 88

Perfect Boiled Noodles 88
Perfect Boiled Rice 89
Pea Cinnamon Noodles 90
Chilli Garlic Noodles 91
Peanut Fried Rice 92
Glass Noodles with Sesame Paste 94
Glutinous Rice 96
Pepper Fried Rice 98

Desserts 99

Toffee Apples 99
Honey Crispies 101

Ingredients used for Chinese Dishes

Mushrooms: There are many varieties which are used in Chinese cooking. To prepare dried mushrooms for cooking, soak them in hot water for ½ hour to soften. Discard any hard stems.

Snow Peas: These are from the pea family and are used in cooking just like we use French beans. These are threaded like French beans and the whole pod is edible. Snap off the stem end of pea pod and pull the string across the pea pod to remove it.

Bamboo Shoots: Fresh tender shoots of bamboo plant are available rarely, but tinned bamboo shoots are easily available in the big stores.

Bok Choy: Bok choy is a variety of Chinese cabbage and is also known as spoon cabbage because the leaves are spoon shaped. This plant has dark green leaves with a white stalk and is an excellent vegetable for stir frying. Both the stalk and the leaves can be used.

Bean Curd or Tofu: Bean Curd or Tofu is prepared from soya bean milk and resembles the Indian Paneer in taste and looks. I have thus substituted it with paneer to give you a few exciting delicacies.

Noodles: Coiled noodles (nest type) called chow are available in small packets in the market or with the vegetable vendors. These are preferred to straight ones. They are usually cooked in boiling water till just done for about 2 minutes only. Never overcook noodles as they turn thick on over cooking.

Rice Noodles: These extremely thin noodles resemble long, transculent white hair. Rice noodles are just soaked in hot water for 10 minutes and then drained before use. When deep fried they explode dramatically into a tangle of airy, crunchy strands that are used for garnish.

Hoisin Sauce: A thick, reddish-brown, sweet and spicy sauce. It's a mixture of soyabeans, plums, garlic, peppers and various spices and is easily available at leading provision stores. In absence of it you can use tomato ketchup, but the taste wont be that good as with hoisin sauce.

Five Spice Powder: This mixture of five ground spices is slightly sweet and pungent. Roast together 2 tsp peppercorns (saboot kali mirch) 3 star anise (phool chakri) 6 laung (cloves) 6" stick dalchini (cinnamon), 3 tsp saunf  (fennel). Grind all the ingredients of the powder in a small mixer to a powder. Strain the powder through a sieve (channi).

Seasoning Cube and Vegetable Stock: Vegetable stock is an important agent for most Chinese soup and sauces. However, if you do not have stock ready or feel lazy to make a stock, you can use seasoning cubes mixed in water instead. Seasoning cubes are available as small packets. These are very salty, so taste the dish after adding the cube before you put more salt. Always crush the seasoning cube to a powder before using it.

STARTERS & DIPS

Kimchi Salad

Serves 4

½ of a medium cabbage - cut into 1½" square pieces
2 tsp salt, 2 tsp sugar, 2 tsp Soya sauce, 1 tsp vinegar, 2 tbsp tomato ketchup
½ tsp salt and ¼ tsp pepper, or to taste, ¼ tsp ajinomotto

GRIND TOGETHER TO A PASTE
2 dry red chillies - deseeded and soaked in water for 10 minutes
1 tsp chopped ginger, 1 tsp chopped garlic

1. Boil 5 cups of water with 2 tsp salt & 2 tsp sugar. Add cabbage to boiling water. Remove from fire. Strain & refresh cabbage in cold water. Leave it in strainer for 15 minutes for water to drain out completely.
2. Drain the red chillies. Grind red chillies with ginger and garlic to a smooth paste using a little water. To the red chilli paste, add Soya sauce, vinegar, tomato ketchup, salt, pepper and ajinomotto.
3. Add the paste to the cabbage and toss lightly so that the paste coats the cabbage. Serve at room temperature.

Crispy Cinnamon Cauliflower

Serves 4

1 small cauliflower - cut into medium florets with long, thin stems (flat pieces)

BATTER
6 tbsp cornflour
4 tbsp plain flour (maida), 4 tbsp suji (semolina)
2-3" stick cinnamon (dalchini) - powdered (1 tsp)
1 tsp garlic - crushed, 1 tsp salt, ½ tsp pepper, ¼ tsp ajinomoto, optional
½ cup water, approx.

RED CHILLI-GARLIC PASTE
3-4 flakes garlic
2 dry red chillies - broken into pieces and deseeded
1" stick cinnamon (dalchini) - broken into pieces

OTHER INGREDIENTS
2 spring onions - chop white and cut greens separately into ¼" pieces diagonally

New Chinese

1 tbsp soya sauce, 1 tbsp tomato sauce
½ tbsp vinegar
½ tsp salt, ¼ tsp ajinomoto

1. Cut cauliflower into medium flat florets. Wash and wipe dry on a clean towel.
2. Make a thick coating batter in a big bowl by mixing all ingredients of batter with a little water.
3. Heat oil in a kadhai for deep frying.
4. Mix cauliflower in the prepared batter nicely. Deep fry half of the cauliflower at a time, on medium flame till golden and cooked. Remove on paper napkins and keep aside.

contd...

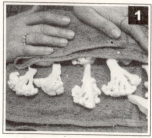

5. For the red chilli - garlic paste, soak all ingredients together in ¼ cup water for 10 minutes and grind to a paste along with the water.
6. Crush dalchini to a powder.
7. Heat 2 tbsp oil in the pan. Add white of spring onions. Stir for a minute till soft.
8. Add red chilli- garlic paste. Stir for ½ minute.
9. Reduce heat. Add soya sauce, tomato sauce and vinegar. Add salt and ajinomoto.
10. Add greens of onions. Mix well.
11. Add ¼ cup water. Stir. Add fried cauliflower and mix well. Serve hot.

New Chinese

Red Sesame Dip

1 tsp saboot dhania - crushed, 2 tsp sesame seeds (til)
3 flakes garlic - chopped, 2 dry red chillies - broken into small pieces, deseeded
4 tbsp ready made tomato puree

ADD LATER
¼ tsp salt, ½ tsp sugar, 1½ tbsp vinegar, ½ tsp soya sauce
1 tsp sesame oil (optional)

1. Heat 2 tbsp oil. Add crushed saboot dhania and sesame seeds. Stir till seeds turn golden.
2. Reduce heat, add garlic and red chillies. Stir till red chillies turn blackish and garlic changes colour.
3. Add tomato puree. Cook for 3-4 minutes or till dry and oil separates. Remove from fire. Let it cool. Put chilli-tomato mixture in a mixer.
4. Add salt, sugar, vinegar, soya sauce and 2 tbsp water to the mixer. Grind all together to a paste. Check salt.
5. Remove to a bowl. Add 1 tsp sesame oil and mix, if using.

Momos

Picture on facing page   Makes 12

DOUGH

1 cup maida (plain flour), 1 tbsp oil, ¼ tsp salt

FILLING

1 onion - finely chopped, 6 mushrooms - chopped finely
1 large carrot - very finely chopped or grated
2 green chillies - finely chopped, 1 tsp ginger-garlic paste
2 cups very finely chopped cabbage (½ small cabbage)
1 tsp salt & ½ tsp pepper powder, or to taste

1. Sift maida with salt. Add oil and knead with enough water to make a stiff dough of rolling consistency, as that for puris.
2. For the filling, heat 2 tbsp oil in the kadhai. Add the chopped onion. Fry till it turns soft. Add mushrooms and cook further for 2 minutes. Add carrot, green chillies and ginger-garlic paste. Mix well and add the cabbage. Stir fry on high flame for 3 minutes. Add salt, pepper to taste. Remove from fire and keep the filling aside.   *Contd...*

3. Make marble sized balls and roll as thin as possible, to make about 5 inch rounds. Put 1 heaped tbsp of the filling. Pick up the sides into loose folds like frills and keep collecting each fold in the centre, to give a flattened ball (like kachorie) shape. Make all momos and keep aside.
4. Place the momos in a greased idli stand or a steamer basket. Fill a large pan with a little water, about 1" at the bottom and place the momos in it. Cover the pan and boil water (steam) on medium flame for about 8-10 minutes. Check with a knife. If the knife is clean, remove from fire. Momos can be had steamed, or can be baked in the oven at 200°C for 5 minutes till light golden on the edges. Serve with chutney given below.

RED HOT CHUTNEY

3-4 dry, Kashmiri red chillies - soaked in ¼ cup warm water, 6-8 flakes garlic
1 tsp saboot dhania (coriander seeds), 1 tsp jeera (cumin seeds), 1 tbsp oil
½ tsp salt, 1 tsp sugar, ½ tsp soya sauce, 3 tbsp vinegar

For the chutney, grind the soaked red chillies along with the water, all the ingredients to a paste.

◁ *Honey Rice Balls: Recipe on page 22*

Honey Rice Balls

Picture on page 20   *Makes 14*

1 cups uncooked rice of short grained quality (permal rice)
2 flakes garlic - crushed (optional), 2 green chillies - chopped finely
¼ cup very finely sliced french beans
1 carrot - finely diced (cut into tiny pieces)
½ big capsicum - diced (cut into tiny pieces)
1½ tsp of salt, ¼ tsp pepper, ¼ tsp ajinomoto (optional)
2 tbsp soya sauce, 3 tbsp honey
1 tbsp vinegar, 1½ tsp chilli sauce
1½ tbsp cornflour

COATING

4 tbsp maida mixed with ½ cup water
1 tsp soya sauce, ¼ tsp salt, a pinch pepper
½ cup sesame seeds (til)

1. Boil 8-10 cups water with 2 tsp salt. Wash and add rice and cook till very soft. Drain rice and keep aside in the strainer.

2. Heat 2 tbsp oil. Reduce heat. Stir fry garlic & green chillies for ½ min.
3. Add beans and carrots. Stir fry for 1 minute. Add capsicum. Mix.
4. Add salt, pepper and ajinomoto. Mix well.
5. Add rice. Sprinkle soya sauce on rice & mix well mashing it in between.
6. Pour honey, vinegar and chilli sauce on the rice and mix well.
7. Sprinkle cornflour and mix well. Remove from fire and let the rice cool down. After it cools down, mash rice well with hands so that it starts to bind and can be formed into a ball.
8. Make marble sized balls with wet hands.
9. Make a thin maida batter by mixing maida with water in a bowl. Add soya sauce, salt and pepper to the batter.
10. Scatter 2 tbsp til on a plate. Do not spread all the seeds at one time.
11. Dip the balls in maida batter and immediately roll over the scattered til. Roll the ball on the til using only the fingers so as to stick the seeds nicely allover the ball. Keep aside till serving time.
12. Deep fry 1-2 balls at a time on medium flame till golden brown and crisp. Remove on paper napkins and serve with red chilli sauce.

Corn Rolls

Cream Style Corn is used in this recipe. In cream style corn, most of the corn kernels are crushed. It is different from tinned corn which has whole kernels.

Picture on page 1 *Makes 8 pieces*

4 pieces of fresh bread

FILLING

1 tin cream style sweet corn, use 1 cup, see note
1 onion - finely chopped
½ tsp garlic paste or 2-3 flakes of garlic crushed to a paste
1 green chilli - deseeded & finely chopped
½ tsp soya sauce, ½ tsp salt, ¼ tsp pepper to taste
½ tsp vinegar
2 tbsp oil

1. Heat oil in a pan, add onion. Cook till onion turns golden.
2. Add garlic paste and green chilli, cook for 1 minute on medium flame.
3. Add 1 cup cream style sweet corn. Mix well.
4. Add soya sauce, salt and pepper and vinegar. Mix well and cook for 2 minutes on medium flame. Remove from fire. Cool.

New Chinese

5. Cut the sides of a slice, keep it flat on a rolling board (chakla).
6. Press, applying pressure with a rolling pin (belan) so that the holes of the bread close. Keep aside. Similarly roll the other slices.
7. Spread a layer of the filling on each bread. Press the filling. Roll the bread carefully.
8. Cut edges of the roll to neaten them.
9. Pan fry/ deep fry each roll in hot oil till golden.
10. Now cut each roll into 2 pieces (straight or diagonally) and serve hot.

Note: The leftover corn, can be stored in an air tight box in the freezer compartment of the fridge for about 2 months or till further use.

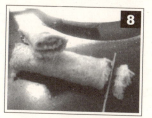

Crunchy Bread Balls

Picture on page 85   *Makes 10 pieces*

1 tbsp chopped onion, 1 tsp grated ginger
1 small green chilli - finely chopped
1 small kheera - peeled, cut into 4 lengthwise, deseeded & chopped very finely
4 tbsp roasted peanuts (moongphali) - crushed
1 potato - boiled and mashed (½ cup)
½ tsp soya sauce
1 tbsp Chinese 5 spice powder (given below)
½ tsp salt or to taste
2 tbsp oil

5 SPICE POWDER
1 tsp peppercorns (saboot kali mirch)
4 star anise (phool chakri)
3 cloves (laung)
3" stick cinnamon (dalchini), 1 tsp fennel (saunf)

OTHER INGREDIENTS
5 white bread slices, oil for deep frying

1. For spice powder, roast all ingredients on a tawa &ground to a powder.
2. Heat 2 tbsp oil in a frying pan, add the onion and ginger. Stir fry for 1 minute.
3. Add the green chilli, kheera and peanuts and stir fry for 2 minutes.
4. Add the mashed potatoes, soya sauce, 5 spice powder and salt. Mix well.
5. Cool, divide into 8 equal balls and keep aside.
6. Remove sides of each bread slice and cut into 2 from the middle.
7. Place one piece of bread in the palm of your hand, put a ball of the potato mixture, press the bread around the ball to cover it completely.
8. Repeat with the remaining balls. Deep fry in hot oil till they turn golden brown. Drain on absorbent paper. Serve hot.

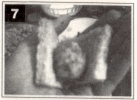
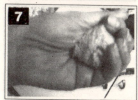

Fried Rice Triangles

Picture on page 37. *Serves 6-8*

6 PANCAKES
¾ cup maida, 1¼ cups milk
a pinch of baking powder, ½ tsp salt, ¼ tsp pepper

FILLING
½ cup uncooked rice - boiled and cooled, deep fried till crisp golden
4 tsp butter, 2 onions - finely chopped
2 tsp ginger-garlic paste or 1" piece ginger & 8-10 flakes of garlic - crushed to a paste
2 tsp soya sauce, 2 tsp vinegar, ¼ tsp ajinomoto
¾ cup coriander - finely chopped, 2-3 spring onion greens only - finely chopped
1 tsp salt and ½ tsp pepper

TO ASSEMBLE
2 tsp red chilli sauce
¼ cup maida dissolved in ½ cup water, 4-5 tbsp oil to fry

New Chinese

1. For the pancakes, mix all ingredients till well blended. Keep aside for 10 minutes. Heat a non stick pan with 1 tsp oil. Remove from fire and pour 1 karchhi full of batter. Rotate the pan gently to spread the batter to a slightly thick pancake of about 5" diameter. Return to fire and cook the pancake till the edges turn light brown. Remove the pancake from the pan, cooking it only on one side. Make 4 such pancakes. Keep on a greased aluminium foil.
2. Boil rice. Let it cool down. Deep fry in medium hot oil till crisp golden. Drain on a paper napkin. Keep aside.
3. Heat butter. Add onions, stir for 2 minutes. Add ginger-garlic paste, soya sauce, vinegar and ajinomoto.
4. Add coriander, greens of spring onions and deep fried rice. Mix well. Add salt and pepper to taste. Remove from fire.
5. Place the pancake on a flat surface, with the brown side up.

Contd...

6. Spread chilli sauce on half of the pancake. Leave the other side of the pancake without any sauce.
7. Spread 2-3 tbsp of the rice mixture on the chilli sauce side.
8. Pick up the side without the filling and fold to get a semi circle. Press well so that the edges stick together. Keep aside.
9. Mix ¼ cup maida with ½ cup water in a flat plate.
10. At serving time, heat 4 tbsp oil in a pan. Dip pancake in maida batter on both sides. Shallow fry one pancake at a time carefully till crisp golden on both sides.
11. Cut each fried pancake semicircle into 3 triangular pieces, sprinkle some grated cheese and dot with sauce. Serve hot.

Final Recipe

New Chinese

Sweet Chilli Dip

A thin dipping sauce which goes well with chinese starters.

3 tbsp sugar, ¼ cup water
1 tbsp honey
1 tsp soya sauce
4 tbsp white vinegar
1-2 tbsp oil
6-8 flakes garlic - crushed to a paste (1 tsp)
½ tsp chilli powder, ¼ tsp salt
1-2 fresh or dry red chillies - very finely chopped or shredded

1. Boil sugar and water till sugar dissolves.
2. Add honey and simmer for 1 minute.
3. Add all other ingredients and remove from fire. Serve.

SOUPS

Fresh Vegetable Stock

Makes 6 cups

1 onion - chopped
1 carrot - chopped, 1 potato - chopped
4-5 french beans - chopped
or
½ cup chopped cabbage
½ tsp crushed garlic - optional
1 tsp crushed ginger, ½ tsp salt
7 cups water

1. Mix all ingredients and pressure cook for 10-15 minutes.
2. Do not mash the vegetables if a clear soup is to be prepared. Strain and use as required.

New Chinese

Quick Vegetable Stock

Soup cubes or seasoning cubes may be boiled with water and used instead of the stock, if you are short of time. These seasoning cubes are easily available in the market and are equally good in taste.

Makes 2½ cups

1 vegetable seasoning cube (maggi, knorr or any other, see note)
2½ cups of water

1. Crush 1 vegetable seasoning cube roughly in a pan.
2. Add 2½ cups of water and give one boil. Use as required.

Note: The seasoning cube has a lot of salt, so reduce salt if you substitute this stock with the fresh stock. Check taste before adding salt.

Lemon Coriander Soup

Serves 4

CLEAR STOCK

5 cups water
1 stick lemon grass - chopped or rind of 1 lemon (1 tsp rind)
¼ cup chopped coriander along with stalks, 1" piece of ginger - sliced
2 laung, 1 tej patta
2 seasoning cubes (maggi or knorr or any other brand)

OTHER INGREDIENTS

½ carrot - peeled and cut into paper thin slices diagonally (¼ cup)
2 mushrooms - cut into thin slices, optional (¼ cup), see picture
1 tsp oil, a pinch of red chilli powder
salt & pepper to taste
2- 3 tbsp lemon juice
¼ tsp sugar
1½ tbsp cornflour dissolved in ¼ cup water
2 tbsp coriander torn roughly with hands

New Chinese

1. If using lemon rind, wash & grate 1 lemon with the peel gently on the grater to get lemon rind. Do not apply pressure and see that the white pith beneath the lemon peel is not grated along with the yellow rind. The white pith is bitter!
2. For stock, mix all ingredients given under stock with 5 cups of water. Bring to a boil. Keep on low flame for 2- 3 minutes. Keep aside.
3. Heat 1 tsp oil in a pan. Add a pinch of red chilli powder.
4. Immediately, add carrot and mushrooms cut into paper thin slices. Saute for 1 minute on medium flame.
5. Add pepper. Check salt and add more if required. Boil.
6. Strain the prepared stock into the vegetables in the pan.
7. Add 1½ tbsp cornflour dissolved in ¼ cup water, stirring continuously.
8. Add lemon juice, sugar and coriander leaves. Simmer for 2 minutes. Add more lemon juice if required. Remove from fire. Serve hot in soup bowls.

Manchow Soup

Serves 6

3 tbsp oil
4 flakes garlic - crushed (½ tsp)
1 tsp very finely chopped ginger
1 cup finely chopped mushrooms (6-8 mushrooms)
1 cup finely shredded (cut into thin, 1" long pieces) cabbage
1½ small carrots - thinly cut into round slices or flowers (1 cup)
salt or to taste
½ tsp pepper, or to taste
a pinch of ajinomoto
3-4 drops of soya sauce, 2 tsp chilli sauce
1 tsp vinegar
2 vegetable seasoning cubes (maggi, knorr or any other)
6 cups water
6 tbsp cornflour dissolved in 1 cup water
½ cup noodles - deep fried till crisp, for garnish, optional

Fried Rice Triangles: Recipe on page 28 ➢

New Chinese

1. Heat 3 tbsp oil. Reduce heat. Add garlic and ginger. Stir on low heat.
2. Add mushrooms. Stir for a minute on medium flame. Add cabbage and carrot. Stir for a minute.
3. Reduce heat. Add pepper, ajinomoto, a few drops soya sauce, chilli sauce and vinegar. Stir to mix well.
4. Add 6 cups water and bring to a boil. Crush 2 seasoning cube and add to the boiling water. Simmer for 2-3 minutes. Check salt and add according to taste.
5. Add dissolved cornflour. Bring to a boil, stirring constantly. Simmer for 2 minutes.
6. Serve in soup bowls, garnished with some crisp fried noodles.

◁ *Mongolian Lotus Stem: Recipe on page 52*

Mushroom Ginger Crispy Rice Soup

Serves 6

½ cup boiled rice - spread on a tray for 10 minutes and deep fried till golden
1 cup sliced fresh mushrooms
1 cup bean sprouts
1 tbsp crushed ginger
6 cups vegetable stock (see page 32) or water with a seasoning cube
1 tbsp soya sauce
1 tbsp vinegar
1 tsp sugar
1 tsp white pepper
salt to taste
¼ tsp ajinomoto (optional)
2 tbsp cornflour dissolved in ¼ cup water
2 tbsp oil

New Chinese

1. Prepare vegetable stock as given on page 32.
2. Slice mushrooms finely.
3. Heat oil. Add mushrooms and bean sprouts. Stir fry for 2 minutes.
4. Add crushed ginger. Stir fry for ½ minute.
5. Add vegetable stock or a seasoning cube (maggi) dissolved in 6 cups of water.
6. Add all the other ingredients except cornflour paste.
7. Boil. Add cornflour paste. Cook for 1 minute till the soup turns thick.
8. Serve soup garnished with fried rice.

Stir Fried Vegetable Soup

Serves 4

1 cup grated cabbage, ½ cup grated carrots
1 tsp oil
1 tsp soya sauce, 2 tsp chilli sauce
½ tsp salt, ½ tsp pepper, or to taste
4 cups vegetable stock *(see page 32 or 33)* or water
3 tbsp cornflour - dissolved in ½ cup water
¼-½ cup paneer - finely diced
2 tbsp lemon juice

1. Grate cabbage and carrot finely.
2. In a pan, heat oil. Add carrot and cabbage. Stir for a minute.
3. Add soya sauce, chilli sauce, salt and pepper. Add 4 cups water. Boil.
4. Dissolve cornflour in ½ cup water, stir well and add the cornflour paste into the soup. Stir till it boils. Remove when the thick.
5. Add some more cornflour dissolved in water, if the soup appears thin.
6. Add tiny cubes of paneer. Add lemon juice and serve hot.

MAIN DISHES

Potato Strings in Ginger Sauce

Serves 4 *Picture on page 48*

2 potatoes
3 capsicums - sliced very thinly to get jullienes (slice in same way as potatoes)
3½ tsp ginger paste of 1½"-2" piece ginger - crushed to a paste
2 onions - chopped
1 tsp salt, ¾ tsp pepper
1 tsp soya sauce, 2 tsp tomato ketchup
2 vegetable seasoning cubes (maggi, knorr or any other)
2¼ tbsp cornflour mixed with ½ cup water

1. To make stock with cube, crush 2 vegetable seasoning cubes and mix with 2 cups of water in a saucepan. Give one boil and keep aside.
2. Peel potatoes and cut each into thin slices, and cut further each slice

Contd...

into very thin fingers to get jullienes. Cut capsicum also in the same way to get thin fingers.

3. Heat oil in a kadhai and deep fry some shredded potatoes at a time. Fry in batches till golden brown and crisp. Drain on paper napkins. Repeat to fry the remaining potato strings.
4. Heat 4 tbsp oil in a kadhai. Add ginger paste. Cook on low flame for 1-2 minutes.
5. Add the chopped onion, cook till golden.
6. Add salt and pepper. Stir fry for a few seconds.
7. Add soya sauce, tomato ketchup and the prepared seasoning water or stock. Give one boil.
8. Add cornflour paste, cook till the sauce just starts to get thick. Remove from fire.
9. At serving time, add fried potatoes and capsicum. Mix well and serve hot immediately.

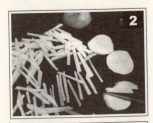

New Chinese

Babycorn Aniseed

Serves 4 *Picture on page 47*

200 gm babycorns

BATTER
3 tbsp cornflour, 2 tbsp plain flour (maida)
2 tbsp suji (semolina)
1 tbsp saunf (aniseeds or fennel) - powdered
½ tsp soya sauce
½ tsp garlic or ginger paste
½ tsp salt
¼ tsp ajinomoto - optional
¼ cup water

RED CHILLI - GARLIC PASTE
1 tsp saunf (fennel seeds)
3-4 flakes garlic
2 dry red chillies - broken into bits and deseeded

OTHER INGREDIENTS

2 spring onions - chop white & cut greens separately into ¼" pieces diagonally

¾ tsp salt

¼ tsp ajinomoto

1 tbsp soya sauce

2 tbsp tomato sauce

½ tbsp vinegar

2 tsp cornflour mixed with ½ cup water

1. Cut a thin slice from the end (not the pointed end) from each baby corn. Wash and wipe well on a clean kitchen towel.
2. Make a thick coating batter by mixing all ingredients of batter with a little water.
3. For the red chilli - garlic paste, soak all ingredients together in ¼ cup water for 10 minutes and grind to a paste along with the water.
4. Heat 3 tbsp oil in a pan. Remove pan from fire and swirl or rotate the pan so as to coat the bottom of the pan nicely with oil. Return to fire.

contd...

Babycorn Aniseed: Recipe on page 45 ➢

5. Dip babycorn in the prepared batter and shallow fry half of the babycorns in a pan on medium flame, turning sides, till golden and cooked. Remove on paper napkins and keep aside.

6. Heat the remaining oil in the pan. Add white of spring onions. Cook for a minute.
7. Add the prepared red chilli- garlic paste. Stir for a minute. Add ¼ cup water. Stir.
8. Reduce heat. Add salt, ajinomoto, soya sauce, tomato sauce and vinegar.
9. Add cornflour paste. Stir for a minute till thick. Add greens of onions and babycorns. Mix well and serve hot.

◄ *Potato Strings in Ginger Sauce: Recipe on page 43*

Cauliflower in Pepper Sauce

Picture on back cover   Serves 2-3

½ of a small cauliflower - cut into ¾" florets (1½ cups)
a pinch of salt, ½ tsp pepper, a pinch of ajinomoto (optional)
greens of 1 spring onion - cut into ½" pieces

SAUCE
1 white portion of spring onion - chopped
¼ tsp ginger paste, ¼ tsp chopped garlic
6 peppercorns (saboot kali mirch)
1 tsp freshly ground black pepper (crush few saboot kali mirch for fresh pepper)
½-1 tsp soya sauce, 1 tsp vinegar
¼- ½ tsp salt or to taste, a pinch of ajinomoto

MIX TOGETHER
1½ cups water
1 vegetable seasoning cube (maggi or knorr)

PASTE
1¾ tbsp cornflour, ¼ cup water

New Chinese

1. Cut cauliflower cut into ¾" florets with a little stalk.
2. Chop white portion of spring onion. Cut the green portion into ½" pieces.
3. Crush 1 vegetable seasoning cubes and add with 1½ cups of water in a saucepan. Give one boil and keep aside.
4. Mix cornflour with water to a smooth paste. Keep aside.
5. Heat 2 tbsp oil in a kadhai and add cauliflower.
6. Stir fry the cauliflower for 3-4 minutes on medium heat till brown specs appear on the cauliflower.
7. Add a pinch of salt, ¼ pepper and pinch of ajinomoto. Keep aside.
8. Heat 2 tbsp oil. Reduce heat and add white of spring onion, ginger paste, garlic and peppercorns. Cook till garlic changes colour. Reduce heat, add black pepper, soya sauce, vinegar, salt and ajinomoto.
9. Add water mixed with a seasoning cube. Give one boil.
10. Add the prepared cornflour paste. Cook till sauce thickens slightly.
11. Add fried cauliflower & greens of spring onion. Remove from fire.

Mongolian Lotus Stem

A sweet and sour lotus stem (bhein) in a Chinese sauce.

Picture on page 38   *Serves 3-4*

200 gm lotus stem (Bhein)

BATTER
4 tbsp cornflour, 4 tbsp plain flour (maida)
½ tsp salt, ¼ tsp pepper
2 flakes garlic - crushed to a paste, ¼ cup water

OTHER INGREDIENTS
2 cups vegetable stock (see page 32) or 2 cups water mixed with 2 vegetable seasoning cubes (maggi)
3 spring onions - white part finely chopped & greens of onions cut into 1" pieces
10 flakes garlic - crushed
6 tbsp tomato ketchup, 1 tbsp vinegar
1 tsp salt or to taste, 1 tsp sugar
2 tbsp cornflour dissolved in ½ cup water

1. Peel lotus stem & cut diagonally into paper thin slices. To parboil lotus stem, boil 4 cups water with

1 tsp salt. Add sliced lotus stem to boiling water. Boil for 2 minutes. Strain. Refresh in cold water. Strain, keep aside.
2. Mix all ingredients of the batter together.
3. Wipe dry the lotus stem with a clean towel. Dip each piece in batter. Deep fry in two batches to a golden yellow colour. Do not brown them. Keep aside.
4. To make stock with cubes, mix 2 veg seasoning cubes with 2 cups of water in a saucepan. Crush cubes. Give one quick boil and keep aside.

5. In a frying pan heat 4 tbsp oil. Add the finely chopped white part of green onions.
6. Add garlic. Remove from fire.
7. Add tomato ketchup, vinegar, salt and sugar.
8. Add the prepared seasoning cube water or vegetable stock. Boil. Simmer for a minute.
9. Add dissolved cornflour to stock, stirring continuously till the sauce just starts to thicken. Keep aside till serving time.
10. At serving time, add the lotus stem and green part of spring onions and cook for 1-2 minutes. Serve hot.

Stir fried Snow Peas/Beans

Picture on page 76   *Serves 4*

200 gms snow peas or french beans
50-75 gm paneer - cut into thin, 2" long pieces
1 onion, 4 tbsp oil
1½" piece ginger - cut into juillenes or thin match sticks (1½ tbsp)
3-4 green chillies - shredded (cut into thin pieces lengthwise)

OTHER INGREDIENTS

1½ tbsp soya sauce
2½ tbsp tomato ketchup
1 tbsp vinegar
1 tsp red chilli sauce
2 tbsp sherry or wine, optional
1½ tbsp worcester sauce
½ tsp salt, ¼ tsp pepper, or to taste
½ tsp ajinomoto (optional)
2 tbsp dry bread crumbs

1. Remove strings/threads from snow peas or beans.

New Chinese

　　If using snow peas, keep whole. If using french beans, cut each into 1½-2" pieces. If using beans, boil 4-5 cups water with 1 tsp salt and 1 tsp sugar. Add beans and boil for 1-2 minutes. Strain.
2. Peel onion. Cut into half and then cut widthwise to get half rings, which when opened become thin long strips and you get shredded onion.
3. Heat oil in pan. Add onion, cook till golden.
4. Add ginger juillenes and green chillies. Stir fry for 1-2 minutes till ginger turns golden.
5. Add snow peas or beans and stir fry for 3-4 minutes till vegetable turns crisp-tender. Keep the vegetable spread out in the pan while stir frying.
6. Reduce heat. Add soya sauce, tomato ketchup, vinegar, red chilli sauce, sherry, worcester sauce, salt, pepper and ajinomoto.
7. Add paneer and mix well.
8. Add bread crumbs. Stir fry on low heat for 2 minutes till the vegetable blends well with the sauces. Serve hot.

Broccoli in Garlic Butter Sauce

Broccoli cooked in a cream sauce with almonds sprinkled on top.

Picture on page 2   *Serves 4*

250 gm (1 medium head) broccoli
½ tsp salt, ½ tsp sugar, 1 tbsp coriander- chopped

SAUCE

¾ cup vegetable stock or 1 veg seasoning cube (maggi or knorr)
3 tbsp butter, 1 onion - sliced
15 flakes garlic - crushed to a paste (1 tbsp)
1 tbsp chopped coriander, 3 tbsp flour (maida), 1 cup milk
2 tsp mustard paste (optional)
½ tsp pepper, ¾ tsp salt, or to taste
1 cup thin cream (if the cream is thick, then thin it down with ¼ cup milk and then measure to get 1 cup thin cream)
TO SPRINKLE - 2 tbsp almonds - chopped

1. To make stock with cube, boil 1 cup water with 1 vegetable seasoning cube. Give one boil and remove from fire. Keep aside.

New Chinese

2. Cut broccoli into medium sized florets with long stalks.
3. Boil 5 cups of water in a large pan. Add 2 tsp salt and 1 tsp sugar to the water. Add broccoli pieces to the boiling water. Bring to a boil. Boil for 1- 2 minutes till crisp tender. Drain. Refresh in cold water. Wipe broccoli well with a clean kitchen towel.

4. In a heavy bottom pan put 3 tbsp butter. Keep on fire and add sliced onions and cook till soft. Add garlic paste. Cook till garlic changes colour.
5. Add boiled broccoli and coriander, stir fry for 2 minutes.
6. Add maida. Stir for 1 minute on medium flame till light golden.
7. Reduce heat. Add milk, stirring continuously.
8. Add prepared stock, mustard paste, pepper and salt. Cook stirring, on low flame till sauce thickens. Remove from fire. Add cream. Keep aside till serving time.

9. At serving time, heat sauce on low heat, serve garnished with almonds.

Steak & Mung Beans

Paneer steaks topped with a semi dry preparation of mung beans and some vegetables.

Picture on page 103   Serves 4-6

200 gms paneer or tofu (take a full block of paneer weighing 200 gms)
4 tbsp oil
2 flakes garlic - crushed
1 tsp grated ginger
1 onion - finely sliced
1 cup mung bean sprouts
½ cup snow peas or 6-8 French beans chopped into ¾" pieces
1 red or yellow capsicum - cut into 1" square pieces
2 tsp sugar
½ tsp salt
¼ tsp pepper
1 tbsp soya sauce
1 tsp cornflour blended with ¼ cup of water

New Chinese

BATTER
3 tbsp cornflour
3 tbsp plain flour (maida)
2 tbsp suji (semolina)
¼ cup ice cold water
2 tbsp chopped coriander
½ tsp salt, ¼ tsp pepper
2 flakes garlic - crushed to a paste

1. Cut whole block of paneer lengthwise into big, flat 4 slices of ¼" thickness. Cut each slice further into 2 pieces from the middle to get 8 square or rectangular pieces, of about 1½" broad.

2. Mix all ingredients of the batter in a bowl. Add just enough water, to make a batter of a thick coating consistency, such that it coats the pieces of paneer.
3. Heat 4 tbsp oil in a pan. Remove from fire and swirl pan (rotate by holding from the handle) to coat the whole bottom of the pan nicely with oil. Return to fire.

Contd...

4. Dip each paneer slice in the batter. Coat on all the sides. Fry in two batches in the pan till well browned and crisp on both sides. Remove from pan and keep aside till serving time.
5. Heat the remaining oil in the pan. Add garlic and ginger and stir-fry for 1 minute.
6. Add sliced onion and stir-fry till onion turns soft.
7. Add bean sprouts and beans or snow peas and yellow or red capsicum. Stir-fry for 1 minute.
8. Add sugar, ½ tsp salt, pepper. Add soy sauce and mix well. Cook for 2-3 minutes.
9. Add cornflour paste. Mix well for 1-2 minutes.
10. To serve, arrange the paneer steaks in a serving platter. Pour the moong beans with vegetables on the steak. Heat in a microwave and serve hot.

New Chinese

Paneer in 5 Spice Powder

A wet dish of crisp fried paneer slices in fragrant spice blend.

Serves 4

200 gms paneer (whole block weighing 200 gms) - cut into ¼" thick rectangular pieces

BATTER
3 tbsp cornflour, 2 tbsp plain flour (maida)
2 tbsp suji (semolina)
½ tsp soya sauce
½ tsp crushed garlic
½ tsp salt, ¼ tsp ajinomoto, optional
¼ cup water, approx.

FIVE SPICE POWDER - ROAST TOGETHER AND GRIND TO A COARSE POWDER (MAKES 6 TSP)
2 tsp peppercorns (saboot kali mirch)
3 star anise (phool chakri), 3 tsp saunf (fennel)
6 laung (cloves), 6" stick dalchini (cinnamon)

OTHER INGREDIENTS

4-5 flakes of garlic - chopped, ½ tsp chopped ginger
½ tsp soya sauce, ½ tbsp vinegar
¼ tsp ajinomoto, ¾ tsp sugar
2 tbsp wine (optional)
2 spring onions - chop white and cut greens separately into ¼" pieces diagonally
2 cups stock or 2 cups water mixed with 1 seasoning cube
2 tbsp cornflour mixed with ½ cup water

1. For five spice powder, grind all the ingredients of the powder in a small mixer to a powder. Strain the powder through a sieve (channi).
2. Cut the block of paneer into rectangular slices of about ¼" thickness. Do not make the slices too thick.
3. Make a thick coating batter by mixing all ingredients of batter with a little water. From the strained spice powder, put 1¼ tsp in the batter. Mix well.

4. Heat 2 tbsp oil in a pan. Remove pan from fire and swirl or rotate the pan so as to coat the bottom of the pan nicely with oil. Return to fire.

5. Dip paneer in the prepared batter and shallow fry half of the paneer in a pan on medium flame till golden crisp on both sides.

6. Remove on paper napkins. Cut each piece of fried paneer diagonally into two to get 2 triangular pieces. Keep aside.

7. Heat 2 tbsp oil in pan. Add white of spring onions and chopped garlic, ginger, remaining five spice powder. Cook till soft.

8. Shut off the flame, add soya sauce, vinegar, ajinomoto, sugar and wine.

9. Return to fire, add 2 cups stock. Give one boil.

10. Add cornflour paste. Stir for a minute till thick. Add fried paneer and chopped spring onion greens. Mix and serve hot.

Kung Pao Corn

Vegetables in a delicious red sauce with corn.

Picture on facing page   Serves 3-4

1 cup tinned corn kernels
1 capsicum - sliced thinly
2 tbsp cashewnuts (kaju)
3 dry, red chillies - keep whole
1 onion - chopped, 1 tbsp ginger - chopped, 1 tbsp garlic - chopped
2 tomatoes - pureed in a mixer
1 tsp soya sauce, 1 tsp red chilli sauce, ½ tsp white vinegar
¼ tsp sugar, ¼ tsp salt or to taste

MIX TOGETHER
2 tsp cornflour, 2 cups water
1 vegetable seasoning cube (maggi)

1. Mix together cornflour, water and seasoning cube. Crush seasoning cube with your hands before mixing it to the water. Mix everything well and keep aside.
2. Slice/slit the kaju from the middle into 2 pieces.

Contd...

New Chinese

3. Heat 2 tbsp oil, add the kaju. Saute until kaju turn golden brown. Remove kaju from oil and keep aside.
4. In the same pan add 1 tbsp oil, reduce heat add dry red chillies, saute for a minute. Do not let them turn black.
5. Add onion and cook till golden.
6. Add the chopped ginger and garlic and saute for a few more seconds.
7. Add pureed tomatoes, soya sauce, red chilli sauce, vinegar, sugar and salt. Cook for about 3-4 minutes till tomatoes turn dry
8. Add corn. Mix well.
9. Stir the above prepared cornflour- cube mixture with a spoon. Add it to the pan. Give one boil. Remove from fire. Keep aside till serving time.
10. At serving time, add the capsicum and the fried kaju. Mix well. Serve.

◁ *Hoisin Stir Fry Okra: Recipe on page 68*

Hoisin Stir Fry Okra

Crispy fried okra (bhindi) tossed in a tempting hoisin sauce.

Picture on page 66   *Serves 4*

250 gms okra (bhindi) - slice into 2 pieces lengthwise
1 onion - cut into 8 pieces
1 tbsp oil, 1 tsp ginger-garlic paste or ½" piece ginger and 3-4 flakes of garlic - crushed to a paste
2 tbsp hoisin sauce or tomato ketchup (use hoisin sauce for better taste)
1 tbsp soya sauce, 2 tbsp red chilli sauce
1 tsp cornflour mixed with ¼ cup water
¼ tsp salt, oil for frying

THIN COATING BATTER
½ cup cornflour, 2 tbsp plain flour
1 tsp ginger-garlic paste
½ tsp salt, ¼ tsp white pepper powder
1 tsp soya sauce, ½ tsp vinegar, 1 tsp lemon juice
¼ cup water to make the batter

1. Remove head of bhindi and cut into 2 long pieces lengthwise.

New Chinese

2. Mix all ingredients of the batter in a big bowl, adding enough cold water (about ¼ to ½ cup) to get a coating batter of pouring consistency. Do not make the batter too thick or too thin.
3. Dip bhindi in batter & mix well. The batter should coat vegetable lightly. If not, sprinkle 2 tbsp more cornflour on the vegetable & mix well.

4. Deep fry in hot oil putting one piece at a time to get crisper bhindis. Do not pick up a handful of pieces to fry together. Add only that much quantity of bhindi which the kadhai can hold (fry in batches). Deep fry till pale golden on medium heat. Remove on paper napkin.

5. Heat 1 tbsp oil in a pan & fry onions for 2 min.
6. Add ginger-garlic paste & saute for ½ a minute.
7. Shut off the flame, add the hoisin sauce, soya sauce, red chilli sauce and ¼ tsp salt. Mix well.

8. At serving time, return to fire and add the fried bhindi and the cornflour paste, mix gently for a minute. Serve immediately.

Half Balls & Veggies in Sauce

Picture on cover Serves 4

BALLS

2 cups cauliflower - grated finely
1 tsp soya sauce
½ tsp salt, ½ tsp pepper
2 tbsp cornflour, 1 tsp ginger/garlic - chopped
2 bread slices - churned in a mixer to get fresh bread crumbs

SAUCE

1 onion - cut into 8 pieces to get 1" squares
1 carrot - cut into thin slices lengthwise, cut each slice diagonally into 1" pieces
1 capsicum - cut into 1" square pieces
10-15 spinach leaves (paalak) - remove stem & keep whole
1 tsp garlic - finely chopped, 1 tsp chopped ginger
½ tsp soya sauce, 1 tsp tomato sauce
2 tsp green chilli sauce, 1 green chilli - chopped
½ tsp vinegar, ½ tsp salt, ¼ tsp pepper
¾ tsp sugar
3 tsp cornflour mixed with 2 cups water

New Chinese

1. Mix all ingredients written under balls. Add fresh bread crumbs churned in a mixer. Mix well and make balls as you do for koftas.
2. Heat oil in a kadhai and deep fry the balls till golden brown.

3. Cut each ball into 2 from the middle and keep aside.
4. Cut carrot into thin slices lengthwise, cut each slice diagonally into 1" pieces.

5. Heat 2 tbsp oil in a pan. Add onion and cook till soft.
6. Add carrot, capsicum and spinach leaves without stem, saute for 2 minutes.
7. Add garlic, ginger, saute for ½ a minute.
8. Remove from fire. Add soya sauce, tomato sauce,

green chilli sauce, chopped green chilli, vinegar, salt, pepper and sugar. Return to fire. Cook sauces for a 10-15 seconds.
9. Add cornflour paste, cook for a few minutes till a thin sauce which coats the spoon is ready. Keep aside till serving time.
10. At serving time, add balls and heat thoroughly and serve immediately.

Billy Kee Mushroom in Sauce

Serves 4

1 packet mushrooms (200 gms)

BATTER

4 tbsp cornflour, 4 tbsp plain flour (maida)
2 tbsp tomato ketchup
2 tbsp chopped coriander
½ tsp salt, ¼ tsp pepper, 2 flakes garlic - crushed to a paste

OTHER INGREDIENTS

1½ tbsp almonds (badam)
1 tbsp chopped garlic, 1 tbsp chopped ginger, 1 green chilli - chopped
3 spring onions - chop greens and white separately
1 cup tomato puree, 1 tbsp soya sauce
½ tsp red wine, optional, 1 tbsp red chilli sauce
1 tsp salt, ¼ tsp ajinomoto
1¼ tsp sugar, 1½ cups water, 2 tbsp cornflour mixed with ¼ cup water

1. Mix all ingredients of the batter in a bowl. Add just enough water, about

New Chinese

     4-5 tbsp, to make a batter of a thick coating consistency, such that it coats the mushrooms.
2. Wash and wipe dry the mushrooms with a clean kitchen towel.
3. Heat 4 tbsp oil in a pan. Remove pan from fire. Swirl the pan (rotate) to coat the bottom of the pan nicely with oil. Return to fire.
4. Dip mushrooms in batter. Pan fry in two batches till crisp brown. Keep aside.
5. Heat the remaining oil in the a pan or wok, add almonds and stir for a minute. Remove from oil and keep aside.
6. Add garlic, ginger and green chilli. Stir for a minute.
7. Add chopped white part of spring onions and cook till soft.
8. Add tomato puree. Mix. Reduce heat. Add soya sauce, red wine, red chilli sauce, salt, ajinomoto and sugar. Stir till it leaves oil.
9. Add ½ of spring onion greens and 1½ cups water. Boil. Simmer for 2-3 minutes.
10. Add the fried mushrooms and fried almonds.
11. Dissolve cornflour in ¼ cup of water and add to the mushrooms. Thicken the sauce a little, stirring continuously. Garnish with the remaining spring onions greens and serve hot.

Moons in Almond Sauce

Picture on facing page   Serves 4

2 cucumbers (kheera), 6-8 almonds (badam)

ALMOND SAUCE
2 tbsp oil
15 almonds (badaam) - ground to a paste with ¼ cup water
1" piece ginger - crushed to a paste (1 tsp)
5-6 flakes garlic - crushed (1 tsp)
2 green chillies - chopped, ½ onion - very finely chopped
1 tbsp soya sauce, 1½ tbsp tomato ketchup
2 tsp vinegar, ½ tsp salt, ¼ tsp pepper
½ bread slice - ground in a mixer to get fresh crumbs

1. Remove bitterness of the cucumber. Peel. Cut lengthwise into two halves. With the help of a scooper or the back of a teaspoon, remove the seeds from the cucumber by pulling the spoon straight down the length of the cucumber half. This way you get a groove in the cucumber piece.

Contd...

New Chinese

2. Cut the cucumber into ½" thick, half-moon slices.
3. Heat 1 tbsp oil in a pan. Add almonds, stir fry for 2-3 minutes till well fried. Remove from pan.
4. In the remaining oil, add cucumber moons (pieces) and stir fry for a minute. Sprinkle a pinch of red chilli powder and some salt. Remove from pan and keep aside.

5. Finely chop the fried almonds.
6. To prepare almond sauce, heat 2 tbsp oil. Reduce heat. Add ginger and garlic. Fry on low flame for 1 minute.
7. Add green chillies and onions. Cook till they turn light brown.
8. Reduce heat and add soya sauce, tomato ketchup, vinegar, salt and pepper. Cook for 1-2 minutes.
9. Add 1½ cups of water. Boil. Keep on slow fire for 2-3 minutes.
10. Add almond paste and fresh bread crumbs. Cook till slightly thick. Keep sauce aside.
11. To serve, boil the sauce. Add the fried cucumber moons (pieces) and the chopped almonds to the sauce. Add ½ tsp more of soya sauce if you like. Keep on slow fire for one minute till heated thoroughly.

◁ *Stir fried Snow Peas/Beans: Recipe on page 54*

Shredded Aubergine in Sweet & Sour Sauce

Serves 6

1 round big aubergine (baingan bharte waala) - peel & cut into ½" thick slices, cut slices into ¾" broad fingers (long, thick pieces)

TOMATO STOCK
2 onions - chopped, 4 big tomatoes - chopped
7-8 flakes garlic - crushed, ¾" piece ginger - chopped
3 cups of water

OTHER INGREDIENTS
3 tbsp oil, 3 onions
2 dry, red chillies - broken into bits
½ tsp white or black pepper, 1½ tsp salt or to taste, ¼ tsp ajinomoto
2 tbsp tomato ketchup, 1 tsp vinegar
½ tsp sugar, ½ tsp soya sauce
4 tbsp cornflour mixed with ¼ cup water

New Chinese

1. Peel baingan and cut into ½" thick slices. Cut slices into ¾" broad fingers. Sprinkle ½ tsp salt on them and keep aside for 20 minutes.
2. Cut each onion into four pieces.
3. For sauce, pressure cook all ingredients for the tomato stock together to give 2-3 whistles.
4. Remove from fire after the pressure drops down. Strain.
5. Keep the tomato stock aside.
6. Heat 3 tbsp oil in a pan. Stir fry onions till soft.
7. Add red chilli pieces, pepper, salt and ajinomoto.
8. Add prepared tomato stock. Give one boil. Reduce the flame.
9. Add tomato ketchup, vinegar, sugar and soya sauce. Boil.
10. Add cornflour mixed with ¼ cup water, stirring continuously.
11. Simmer for 1-2 minutes till thick.
12. Heat oil in a kadhai. Deep fry baingan till tender. Drain on napkin. Keep aside.
13. At the time of serving, add fried aubergine fingers and heat for a minute.

Veggies in Caramelized Sauce

Serves 4-5

1 packet (100 gm) babycorns - keep whole
20- 22 leaves of spinach - chop stem and roughly tear each leaf into 2 by hand
2-3 dry, red chillies - broken into pieces, deseeded & ground to a rough powder
¼ tsp salt
5 tbsp chopped walnuts (akhrot)

CARAMELIZED SAUCE
2 tsp butter, 2 tsp sugar
2 medium onions - chopped, 1 tsp chopped garlic
a drop of soya sauce, a pinch of ajinomoto, 2 tsp vinegar
2 vegetable seasoning cubes (maggi, knorr or any other brand)
5 tbsp cornflour

1. To make stock with cube, boil 4 cups water with 2 vegetable seasoning cubes. Give one boil and remove from fire. Keep aside.
2. Dissolve cornflour in ¼ cup of water and keep aside.
3. Heat 5 tbsp oil in a wok or a kadhai, add dry red chilli powder, stir fry for a minute.

4. Add babycorns and cook covered for 4-5 minutes on medium heat till brown specs appear on the babycorn and they get crisp-tender.

5. Add spinach and stir fry for another 1-2 minutes. Add ¼ salt. Remove from fire.
6. For sauce, heat 2 tsp butter in a pan on low heat, let it get light brown, add 2 tsp sugar, let it melt, wait for a few seconds more till it turns golden.

7. Add chopped onion and chopped garlic. Cook till onion turn soft.
8. Reduce heat, add soya sauce, ajinomoto and vinegar. Mix
9. Add the prepared stock (water mixed with seasoning cube). Bring to a boil.
10. Add cornflour mixed with water. Stir till sauce thickens slightly.
11. Add stir fried babycorn, spinach and chopped walnuts. Mix well, remove from fire. Serve hot.

Garlic Honey Cottage Cheese

Serves 3-4

100 gms cottage cheese (paneer) - cut into 1" cubes and deep fried
a 3-4" piece of cabbage - cut into 1½" squares (1 cup)
1 small onion - cut into 4 pieces and separated
½ tsp freshly ground pepper, ½ tsp salt, or to taste
2 tsp red chilli sauce, 1 tbsp tomato sauce
1 tbsp soya sauce
2 tsp honey
½ tbsp vinegar
3 tbsp cornflour mixed with ¼ cup water
2-3 tbsp oil

GRIND TOGETHER

4 dry red chillies - remove seeds, break into small pieces & soak in water for 10 minutes
12-15 flakes garlic
1 tsp vinegar
¼ tsp jeera (cumin), 2-3 saboot kali mirch (peppercorns)

New Chinese

1. Soak dry red chillies. Drain and grind to a paste with garlic, vinegar, jeera and saboot kali mirch. Keep aside.
2. Cut cabbage into 1½" square pieces. Cut onion into fours and separate the slices.
3. Dissolve cornflour in ¼ cup water and keep aside.
4. Heat oil in a kadhai. Reduce heat and add prepared red chilli and garlic paste.
5. Stir and add onion. Mix. Add cabbage. Stir for 3-4 minutes. Add pepper and salt.
6. Stir. Reduce heat. Add red chilli sauce, tomato sauce, soya sauce, honey & vinegar.
7. Add paneer and mix well for 2 minutes.
8. Pour 1½ cups of water and bring to a boil. Lower heat.
9. Add the dissolved cornflour and cook till the sauce turns thick. Serve hot.

Schzewan Vegetables

Garnish these vegetables in hot sauce with deep-fried rice noodles if you like.

Serves 3-4

1 medium sized onion - cut into 8 pieces
1 medium sized carrot - cut into thin rounds
8 french beans - cut into 1" pieces
5 babycorns - cut diagonally into 2 pieces
¼ of a small cucumber (kheera) - cut into round slices and halved
1 capsicum - cut into 8 pieces

MIX TOGETHER
1 tbsp oil, 3 tsp cornflour
2 dry red chillies - break into very small pieces and remove seeds
¼ tsp chilli powder, 3 laung (cloves) - crushed, 8 flakes garlic - crushed
3 tbsp vinegar, 2 tsp sugar, 2 tsp soya sauce, 2 tsp tomato ketchup
½ tsp salt, ¼ tsp pepper, 1 tsp sherry or rice wine (optional)
2 cups stock (page 32) or 2 cups water mixed with 1 veg seasoning cube

Crunchy Bread Balls: Recipe on page 26 ➢

New Chinese

Chilli Garlic Noodles

Serves 4

100 gm noodles - boiled
1 tsp garlic paste or 3-4 flakes of garlic - crushed to a paste
3 dry, whole red chillies - broken into bits
½ tsp red chilli flakes or powder
½ tsp salt or to taste
½-1 tsp soya sauce

1. To boil noodles, **see page 88.**
2. Wash with cold water several times. Strain. Leave them in the strainer for 15-20 minutes, turning them upside down, once after about 10 minutes to ensure complete drying.
3. Apply 1 tsp oil on the noodles and spread in a tray, till further use.
4. Heat 3 tbsp oil. Add garlic paste, cook till golden.
5. Remove from fire, add broken red chillies and red chilli flakes or powder.
6. Return to fire and mix in the boiled noodles. Add salt and a little soya sauce. Do not add too much soya sauce.
7. Mix well for 2-3 minutes with help of 2 forks. Serve hot.

Peanut Fried Rice

Serves 3-4

1½ cups uncooked rice
3 tbsp oil
4 flakes garlic - crushed (optional)
2 green chillies - chopped finely
2 green onions - chopped till the greens, keep greens separate
1 tsp salt, 1 tsp pepper, ¼ tsp ainomoto (optional)
½ tsp soya sauce (according to the colour desired), 1 tsp vinegar (optional)
½ tsp tomato ketchup

GRIND TOGETHER TO A PASTE
3 tbsp roasted peanuts (moongphali)
5½ tbsp milk

FOR GARNISHING
2 tbsp roasted peanuts - roughly crushed on a chakla belan

1. To boil rice, **see page 89.**
2. Grind all ingredients of paste to a smooth paste.

New Chinese

3. Chop spring onions till the greens, keep white and green separately.
4. Heat oil. Stir fry garlic, green chillies and white of onions.
5. Add peanut paste. Mix. Reduce heat, add salt, pepper and ajinomoto, soya sauce, vinegar and tomato ketchup. Mix.
6. Add boiled rice and green portion of spring onions. Mix and stir fry the rice for 2 minutes with the help of 2 forks. Remove from fire.
7. Serve hot garnished with crushed roasted peanuts.

Glass Noodles with Sesame Paste

Glass noodles are thin long translucent noodles. In the absence of these the regular noodles or rice seviyaan can be used. Boil the regular noodles for 2 minutes where as the glass noodles or the rice seviyaan just needs to be soaked in hot water for 5 minutes.

Picture on page 1   Serves 6

100 gms glass noodles or rice seviyaan
2 tbsp oil
3 spring onions - cut into rings, till the greens, keep white separate

SESAME PASTE (GRIND ALL TOGETHER)
3 tbsp sesame seeds (til) - soak for 10 minutes in 5 tbsp hot milk & 2 tbsp water and then grind to a paste
½ tsp red chilli powder or to taste, ¾ tsp salt
4 flakes garlic - finely chopped
1½ tbsp soya sauce, ½ tsp sugar

1. Cut white spring onion into rings till the greens.

— **New Chinese**

2. In a large pan, boil 8 cups water with 1 tsp salt and 1 tsp oil. Remove from fire. Add noodles to hot water. Cover and keep aside for 5 minutes in hot water. Drain.

3. Wash with cold water several times. Strain. Leave them in the strainer for 15-20 minutes, turning them upside down, once after about 10 minutes to ensure complete drying. Apply 1 tsp oil on the noodles and spread on a large tray. Dry the noodles under a fan for 15-20 minutes. Keep aside till further use.

4. Grind all ingredients of til paste to a smooth paste.
5. Heat oil in a pan, remove from fire. Swirl the pan to coat the bottom of the pan nicely with oil. Add white of spring onions, stir for a minute.

6. Add prepared til mixture, mix well and stir for 2 minutes on low heat.
7. Add noodles, mix well. Add spring onion greens. Mix and serve hot.

Glutinous Rice

A sticky rice dish! It's a little sweet because of the honey added to it. Do try it.

Serves 6

1½ cups uncooked rice (ordinary quality short grained rice, permal chaawal)
2 tbsp oil
1 onion - sliced
2 flakes garlic - crushed
2 spring onions - chop white and green part separately
2 green chillies - chopped
½ cup peas (matar)
½ tsp jeera powder (cumin powder), ½ tsp dhania powder (ground coriander)
1 tsp saunf - crushed
1 tsp salt, ½ tsp pepper

MIX TOGETHER
3 cups veg stock or 3 cups of water mixed with 1 vegetable seasoning cube
2 tbsp honey
2 tbsp soya sauce

1. Wash and soak rice. Keep aside.
2. Mix all the ingredients written under mix together in a bowl. Keep aside.
3. Heat oil in a large deep pan, add sliced onion and garlic and stir-fry for 4-5 minutes or until onion is soft.
4. Add white part of spring onion, green chillies and peas.
5. Add jeera powder, dhania powder, crushed saunf, salt and pepper. Stir-fry for 1 minute.
6. Drain rice and add to the pan. Stir for 3-4 minutes on low heat.
7. Add stock-honey mixture and green of spring onion. Stir and bring to a boil.
8. Reduce heat and cook covered for 10 minutes or until rice is done and the water gets absorbed. Serve hot.

Final Dish

Pepper Fried Rice

Serves 3-4

1½ cups uncooked rice
5 saboot kali mirch (whole peppercorns)
3 flakes garlic - crushed & chopped (optional)
2 green chillies - chopped finely
2 green spring onions
2 carrots - grated and squeezed well
1 tsp salt or to taste
1½ tsp freshly crushed peppercorns
½ tsp ajinomoto (optional), ½ tsp vinegar

1. To boil rice, **see page 89.**
2. Chop spring onions till the greens, keep greens and white separately.
3. Heat 3 tbsp oil in a pan/kadhai. Add saboot kali mirch, garlic, green chillies and white of onions. Cook for a minute.
4. Add grated carrot, salt, pepper and ajinomoto. Cook for ½ a minute.
5. Add rice and vinegar. Mix gently.
6. Add green onions. Stir fry the rice for 2 minutes. Serve hot.